Time to Get Ready

Teaching Kids About Salvation and the End of Time

Shannon Scott
Illustrations by Ron Wheeler

Copyright © 2015 Shannon Scott
Copyright © 2015 TEACH Services, Inc.
ISBN-13: 978-1-4796-0460-9 (Paperback)
ISBN-13: 978-1-4796-0461-6 (iBooks)
ISBN-13: 978-1-4796-0462-3 (Kindle Fire)
Library of Congress Control No: 2014960315

TEACH Services, Inc.
P U B L I S H I N G
www.TEACHServices.com • (800) 367-1844

Jesus made Adam and Eve on the sixth day, and then He celebrated the Sabbath with them on the seventh day. It was a very special day of worship and rest, unlike the other six days of work. They must have spent the whole day together singing, talking, eating, and walking through the beautiful Garden of Eden.

Just like Jesus made Adam and Eve, He made you too, and He wants to spend Sabbath with you as well.

Although we can't walk in the garden with Jesus in person, we can spend time with Him by:

going to church,
singing songs about His love,
reading Bible stories,
helping others,
and enjoying the beautiful
world He created.

The Sabbath was God's first gift to us, but His best gift was His Son. God sent His Son to the earth to save us from our sins.

When we do bad things, we sin, and the Bible tells us that when we sin, we grow farther away from Jesus. In order to fix our sin problem, Jesus lived a perfect life and then died for us.

His death gives us salvation. All we need to do is love Jesus and be His friend. When we do that, we will want to ask forgiveness for our sins and obey His commandments.

After Jesus was raised from the dead, He spent forty days with His friends. During that time He talked to them about the future. He told them He was going back to heaven to build beautiful houses and that He would come back soon. He also told them that bad people would do mean things to them and would make rules that would go against God's Word.

Jesus told His friends about heaven and the end of the world because He wanted them, and us, to be prepared.

Jesus is coming very soon to take us to heaven. We don't know the exact date, but the Bible tells us it will happen very soon.

And we want to be ready!

You see, right before Jesus comes a lot of things are going to happen.

The Bible tells us that some people are going to make a law that says we can't go to church on Sabbath.

Remember, the Sabbath is important because in the fourth commandment God asks us to remember the Sabbath and worship Him on His special day.

When we obey His commandments and keep the Sabbath, it shows Jesus how much we love Him, just like we show Mommy and Daddy that we love them when we obey them.

When that law is made, it will be hard to buy food and other things because we go to church on Sabbath, so we might have to move to the country or go to the mountains where we can grow our own food.

It might be a little scary, but we don't need to worry because Jesus has promised to take care of us and always be with us.

And even if Mommy and Daddy aren't with you, you can talk to Jesus because He loves you even more than they do!

People may try to trick you into disobeying Jesus, but it's important to remember to follow Him no matter what.

His way is the best way, and when we follow God's word, we will be ready to meet Jesus when He comes again.

It will be so exciting
when Jesus comes
in a big white cloud
with beautiful angels to take us
to live with Him forever.

Heaven is going to be amazing!

We won't get hurt there. The animals
won't bite. Nothing will scare us.
We'll get to be with our family.
And everyone will be happy.

Of course, the best part is
that we'll be with Jesus.
He can't wait to spend time with you!

We invite you to view the complete
selection of titles we publish at:

www.TEACHServices.com

Scan with your mobile
device to go directly
to our website.

Please write or e-mail us your praises, reactions, or
thoughts about this or any other book we publish at:

TEACH Services, Inc.
P U B L I S H I N G
www.TEACHServices.com ● (800) 367-1844

P.O. Box 954
Ringgold, GA 30736

info@TEACHServices.com

TEACH Services, Inc., titles may be purchased in bulk for
educational, business, fund-raising, or sales promotional use.
For information, please e-mail:

BulkSales@TEACHServices.com

Finally, if you are interested in seeing
your own book in print, please contact us at

publishing@TEACHServices.com

We would be happy to review your manuscript for free.